NATIVE NATIONS OF NORTH AMERICA

Life of the Powhatan

Rebecca Sjonger & Bobbie Kalman

Crabtree Publishing Company

www.crabtreebooks.com

Life of the Powhatan

Created by Bobbie Kalman

Dedicated by Rebecca Sjonger
For Bruce, Gael, Jonathan, Julianne, and Adrienne Miller

Editor-in-Chief
Bobbie Kalman

Writing team
Rebecca Sjonger
Bobbie Kalman
Kathryn Smithyman

Substantive editors
Amanda Bishop
Deanna Brady

Editors
Molly Aloian
Kristina Lundblad
Kelley MacAulay

Art director
Robert MacGregor

Design
Katherine Kantor

Production coordinator
Katherine Kantor

Photo research
Crystal Foxton

Consultant
Dr. Jon Parmenter, Department of History, Cornell University

Photographs and reproductions
Ashmolean Museum, University of Oxford: page 23
The Granger Collection, New York: pages 7, 26, 27
Jack Paluh Arts, www.jackpaluh.com, 1-814-796-4400: page 19 (bottom)
The Mariners' Museum, Newport News, VA: front cover, title page,
    pages 11, 13, 17, 18
Nativestock.com: pages 12, 14, 15, 16
© North Wind Picture Archives: pages 28, 29
www.powhatan.org: page 31
Used with permission from THROUGH INDIAN EYES,
    copyright © 1995 The Reader's Digest Association, Inc.,
    Pleasantville, New York, www.rd.com. Illustration by Craig
    Nelson.: pages 8-9
Ann Thiermann, www.annthiermann.com: page 25
Valentine Richmond History Center: page 30
Other images by Corel, Digital Stock, and Digital Vision

Illustrations
Barbara Bedell: pages 16, 19 (top), 22 (right), 24
Katherine Kantor: border, pages 4 (main map), 6, 20, 21, 22 (left)
Margaret Amy Reiach: back cover (hide background),
    title page (background)
Bonna Rouse: back cover (village), page 4 (inset map)

Crabtree Publishing Company

www.crabtreebooks.com   1-800-387-7650

Copyright © **2005 CRABTREE PUBLISHING COMPANY**.
All rights reserved. No part of this publication may be
reproduced, stored in a retrieval system or be transmitted in
any form or by any means, electronic, mechanical, photocopying,
recording, or otherwise, without the prior written permission
of Crabtree Publishing Company. In Canada: We acknowledge the
financial support of the Government of Canada through the Book
Publishing Industry Development Program (BPIDP) for our
publishing activities.

Cataloging-in-Publication Data
Sjonger, Rebecca.
  Life of the Powhatan / Rebecca Sjonger & Bobbie Kalman.
    p. cm. -- (Native nations of North America series)
  Includes index.
  ISBN 0-7787-0380-0 (RLB) -- ISBN 0-7787-0472-6 (pbk.)
  1. Powhatan Indians--History. 2. Powhatan Indians--Social life and
customs. 3. Pocahontas, d. 1617 I. Kalman, Bobbie. II. Title.
III. Native nations of North America.
  E99.P85S56 2005
  975.004'97347--dc22
                                                    2004012800
                                                         LC

**Published in
the United States**
PMB16A
350 Fifth Ave.
Suite 3308
New York, NY
10118

**Published
in Canada**
616 Welland Ave.,
St. Catharines, Ontario
Canada
L2M 5V6

**Published in the
United Kingdom**
73 Lime Walk
Headington
Oxford
OX3 7AD
United Kingdom

**Published
in Australia**
386 Mt. Alexander Rd.,
Ascot Vale (Melbourne)
VIC 3032

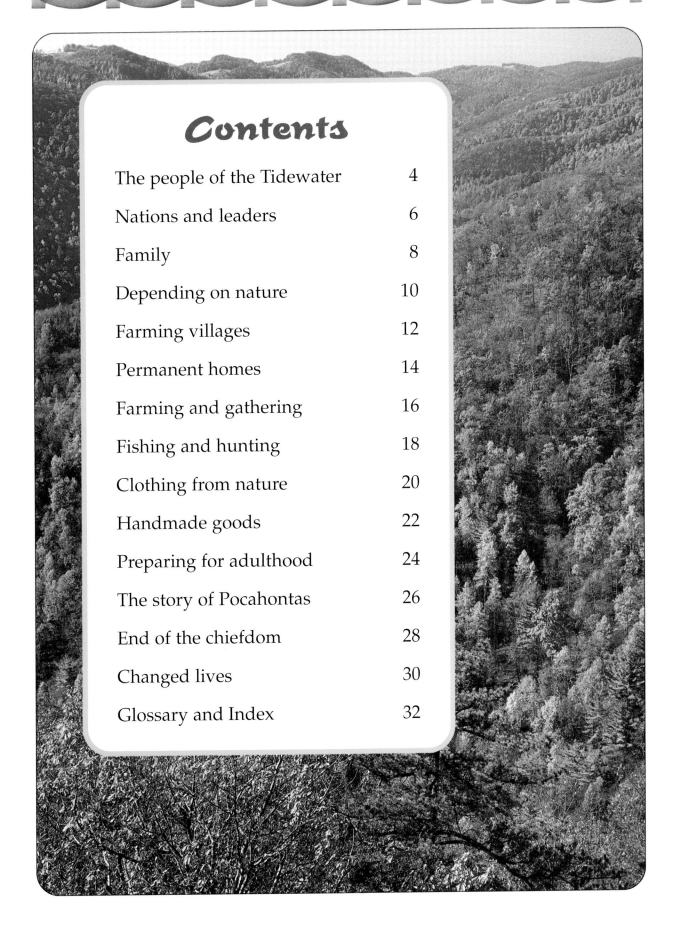

Contents

The people of the Tidewater

For thousands of years, **indigenous**, or Native, people have lived in the Tidewater region of present-day Virginia. The region is bordered by the Atlantic Ocean to the east. The region stretches west onto the **coastal plain**, which is an area of flat land that extends from the shoreline. The region is crisscrossed with waterways, including many rivers that flow into Chesapeake Bay. At first, the Native people in the region were hunter-gatherers who moved from place to place in search of food. Over time, the people began farming the land around them. They built permanent villages in which they lived year-round.

The nations unite

The people who settled in villages in the Tidewater region belonged to many **nations**. Nations are groups of people who share origins, customs, languages, and leaders. By the early 1600s, most of the Native nations in the region united under a powerful leader named Wahunsonacock. Some people called these nations a **confederacy**, which is a group of nations that join together and have equal power. Wahunsonacock had great power over the nations, however. He ruled the nations as a **chiefdom**, or a group under the authority of one leader.

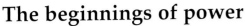

The beginnings of power

In the 1500s, Wahunsonacock's **ancestors** created a confederacy of about six neighboring nations, including the Powhatan, the Mattaponi, and the Pamunkey nations. Wahunsonacock inherited leadership of this confederacy.

He took the position of **paramount**, or highest, chief in the late 1500s and formed a chiefdom. Over time, he added nations to the chiefdom. By 1607, there were over 30 nations under his command. The people called their **territory** "Tsenacommacah," which meant "densely inhabited land."

The Powhatan name

Wahunsonacock took as his personal title the name of his favorite village, where he had grown up. The village was called Powhatan, and he called himself Powhatan. The English **settlers** who arrived in the Tidewater region in 1607 came from a country that had a king. They sometimes spoke of Chief Powhatan as the "king" of his people. Later, they called all the people in his chiefdom the Powhatan people. The nations in the chiefdom spoke one language, which also became known as Powhatan. The language belonged to the Algonquian **language family**.

The village of Powhatan was named for a nearby waterfall. The word "powhatan" means "waterfall."

Nations and leaders

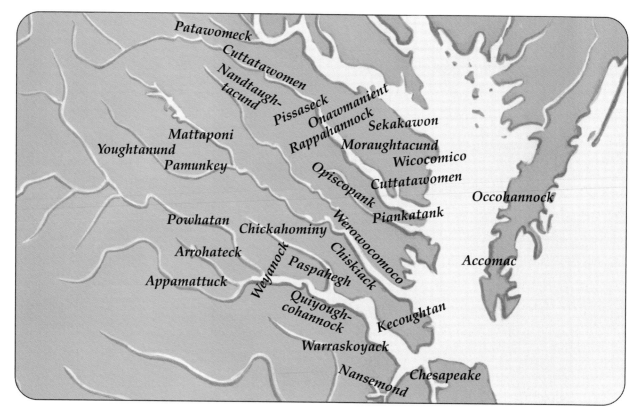

Patawomeck
Cuttatawomen
Nandtaugh-tacund
Pissaseck
Onawmanient
Rappahannock
Sekakawon
Mattaponi
Youghtanund
Pamunkey
Moraughtacund
Wicocomico
Opiscopank
Cuttatawomen
Occohannock
Powhatan
Chickahominy
Werowocomoco
Piankatank
Arrohateck
Chiskiack
Accomac
Weyanock
Paspahegh
Appamattuck
Quiyough-cohannock
Kecoughtan
Warraskoyack
Nansemond
Chesapeake

Some nations became part of the Powhatan chiefdom when they lost battles against Powhatan nations. Wahunsonacock increased the size of his territory and the loyalty of his people even more by marrying women from many nations in the Tidewater region. His wealth and power increased as the size of his chiefdom increased. The Powhatan nations were expected to provide him with **tributes**, or gifts, every year. They sent him many valued items, including crops and animal **hides**, or skins. In return, the nations received protection and higher status as members of the chiefdom. The map above shows the nations that were part of the Powhatan chiefdom in the early 1600s.

Separate nations

Each Powhatan nation kept its own name and distinct identity. The people of each nation also controlled the areas where they traditionally lived and found food. The farther away a nation was from Werowocomoco—the capital village and center of Wahunsonacock's power—the less influence the chief had over that nation.

Similar lifeways

The daily **lifeways** of the people who lived in the region were similar. They all depended on the same resources from nature to build shelters, feed themselves, and make clothing and other goods. They also shared similar cultures and traditions.

Werowances

Wahunsonacock was the *mamanatowick*, or paramount leader, of the Powhatan chiefdom. Each nation also had its own chief called a *werowance*. The daily lives and duties of many werowances were similar to those of the people they ruled over, but werowances were often wealthier and had higher status. Werowances usually inherited their positions **matrilineally**, or through their mothers' families. Spiritual leaders and war leaders also held positions of power. They helped werowances make decisions about important issues. Wahunsonacock strengthened his own power by replacing leaders he did not trust with loyal relatives and friends.

Leadership roles

As werowances gained power, their wealth and status also increased. Many leaders received tributes, such as copper jewelry, from the members of their nations. In addition to governing their people, werowances were sometimes war chiefs. Werowances often led seasonal festivals, as well as spiritual ceremonies. They were the keepers of the traditional lands of their nations. Each nation's werowance participated in **councils**, or meetings, with other werowances. Since leadership was inherited matrilineally, some of the werowances were women who had no brothers to act as chiefs. Female leaders were called *weroansqua*.

As the paramount leader, Wahunsonacock had complete power over his werowances.

Family

Family was extremely important to Powhatans. **Extended families** lived together. Extended families included grandparents, aunts, uncles, and cousins who lived with a married couple and their children. Family members took care of one another and shared everything, including their homes, food, entertainment, and daily chores.

Marriage

For men, marriage was a sign of responsibility. They could not take part in council meetings until after they were married. When a man was interested in marrying a woman, he offered many gifts—both to her and to her parents! The gifts were items, such as cooking utensils and food, which were needed to set up a home. A man gave gifts to show that he could provide for his wife. If two families agreed on a match between their children, they sprinkled shell beads over the heads of the young couple and held a feast to celebrate the marriage. A new wife left her own family and joined her husband in his family's home. The couple's children were part of the husband's mother's household.

Werowances were honored among the people they led. A werowance could marry any woman from his nation. Wahunsonacock had many wives, who came from all over his chiefdom.

Depending on nature

Many large and small waterways run through the Tidewater region. In the early 1600s, thick forests grew over the whole area. Plenty of useful materials were available in the waters and forests. People knew where to find everything they needed to survive in each season. They were very creative and used plants, shells, stones, and animal parts in many ways. They made these materials into homes, food, clothing, and other important goods.

Trade

Most of the Powhatan nations had access to the same materials from nature within their territories. The neighboring nations that lived to the north, south, and west of the Powhatan chiefdom did not have the same resources, however. The Powhatans traded sought-after goods that were plentiful in the Tidewater region in exchange for items not found there. For example, they exchanged dried oysters for the copper offered by traders from nations to the west.

Riding the rivers

People traveled from place to place on the many rivers that ran through the Tidewater region. They made dugout canoes called *quintans* to transport people and goods between their villages and territories.

Never wasteful
The Powhatans were careful to take only what they needed from nature. Hunters never caught more animals than were needed by the people of their villages. The animals that were brought back to the villages were not wasted. For example, a deer's hide was made into bedding, clothing, and footwear. Its **sinews** made strong thread for stitching together pieces of hide. Every scrap of the deer meat became part of a meal. The animal's bones and antlers were crafted into tools and utensils. People were thankful to the animals that gave up their lives to provide so many useful items!

Making a canoe

To create a quintan, men went into the woods to select a large tree to cut down and bring back to the village. Once the log was laid down, small sections of it were set on fire. Chunks of the charred wood were scraped out with shells until there was a hollowed-out area for seating and storing goods. Finished canoes could hold ten to forty people. Branches and small pieces of wood were carved into paddles or poles that moved the canoe through the water.

Farming villages

The Powhatans lived throughout the Tidewater region in about 200 villages of varying sizes. Most of the villages were built on riverbanks so that people could easily fish and travel by canoe. Some of the rivers in present-day Virginia still bear the names of the nations that once lived along them. The soil near rivers was good for farming, which was a main source of food for the Powhatans. Each nation's werowance usually lived in the largest or wealthiest village in his or her territory. Some large villages were made up of over 1,000 people living in up to 50 homes. In addition to homes, large villages had places where people held ceremonies. Villages also had storage buildings for tributes and other goods and workshops for repairing tools and weapons. Smaller villages had as few as ten homes. Many communities were protected by **palisades**, or walls of wooden poles that were sharpened into points at their tops. Villagers guarded their homes from enemy attacks by watching for strangers from the high ground of the riverbanks.

Time to move

Powhatan villages were mainly farming communities. Each village was surrounded by vegetable gardens and fields of planted crops. The people planted crops in different fields each year. The unplanted fields were allowed to go wild for one season so the soil could regain its **nutrients** for future crops. As villages grew, some resources, such as nearby trees, were used up. When resources were used up, entire villages sometimes moved to new areas.

Temporary camps

At various times during the year, small groups of fishers, hunters, and gatherers left their villages and traveled to traditional areas where they collected foods. As they traveled around their territories, they set up small **temporary**, or short-term, camps. People fished, hunted, or gathered during the day and returned to the camps at night. They did not remain in the camps for long. After collecting the food they needed, they returned home.

Permanent homes

The Powhatan people called their homes *yi-hakans*. The structures were similar to the **longhouses** that were built by other nations in the areas surrounding the Tidewater region. Yi-hakans were rounded on all sides to make them wind-resistant. Each yi-hakan was home to as many as 20 people. Large extended families and the families of werowances usually had an entire yi-hakan to themselves.

Building a yi-hakan

Women owned and built the yi-hakans. Most yi-hakans could be built in less than a day, but collecting the materials needed to make them took much longer. Women spent many months gathering items such as **saplings**, bark, and plants before they could begin assembling a yi-hakan. After stripping the branches from saplings, they tied the saplings together to make a frame for the building. They then bent the saplings into a dome shape and covered the frame with mats woven from reeds and **plant fibers**, or the threadlike parts of plants. The mats were also used as flaps that covered doorways. Some families added bark coverings to their yi-hakans to make them even sturdier.

Inside a yi-hakan

There was plenty of room inside a yi-hakan for families to sit, cook, eat, rest, and store goods. Items such as tools and weapons were stored on platforms or hung from the sapling frame. Food was also kept in a yi-hakan for protection from the weather and wild animals. Wooden sleeping platforms were built into the sides of the structure. Comfortable bedding was made from animal hides and plant-fiber mats.

Protective shelters

A yi-hakan was designed to protect the inside living space from wind, sun, rain, and snow throughout the year. Rain and snow slid off the curved roofs. The mats that covered a yi-hakan were woven with small openings that allowed fresh air to flow into the home in summer. In winter, extra mats were piled on top of the yi-hakan to trap the warm air inside.

Around the fire

Each yi-hakan had a fire pit at its center. Wood and corncobs were used to fuel the fire, which was used for cooking and also for keeping people warm in winter. Families gathered around the fire pit to eat, socialize, and tell stories. An opening in the top of the yi-hakan allowed some smoke to escape, but people were used to the smoky air that filled their homes. In summer, it helped keep out mosquitoes!

Farming and gathering

Women were in charge of the farming activities in their communities. They used tools made from animal bones, wood, and stones. In spring, they prepared the gardens and carefully planted seeds. During summer and early fall, the farmers harvested many crops, including corn, beans, squash, pumpkins, and sunflowers. Traditionally, Powhatans shared the foods they grew. Farmers gave the outer row of vegetables to wild animals and shared the next row with people who did not have enough food of their own. They then used the inner rows of crops to feed their families.

In addition to growing their own food, women gathered wild plants, fruits, seeds, and nuts. They knew where to collect hundreds of types of wild plants that could be eaten or used in medicines. Gathering trips took Powhatan women all over the region. The women searched in forests and swampy areas where these plants were plentiful. They transported large loads of food back to their villages in dugout canoes.

Year-round supplies

The Powhatans ate some of the farmed and gathered foods when they were fresh. The rest of the food was saved and **preserved**, or prepared so it would not spoil. Women dried out many vegetables and fruits by baking them on flat rocks placed in a fire or in the hot sun. They pounded dried corn until it became coarse flour that was used to make bread. They stored the preserved foods in containers until the foods were needed to make stews or soups.

Giving thanks

Powhatan people believed that foods such as corn, beans, and squash were gifts from their creator. They held seasonal ceremonies to honor the creator and the spirits. For example, a ceremony that included dancing, feasting, and forgiving enemies was held every summer to give thanks for the corn harvest.

Fishing and hunting

Powhatan women were skilled farmers and gatherers, and Powhatan men were expert fishers and hunters. A steady supply of fish, birds, and animals caught by the men was added to the assortment of plant foods provided by the women. Fishers and hunters were busy finding food in every season.

Fishing

The rivers and streams in the Tidewater region provided Powhatan fishers with excellent sources of food. The wildlife found in the waterways included turtles, clams, and fish, such as trout and bass. Fishers used a variety of tools to assist them with their jobs. They sometimes used fish hooks made from animal bones, which were attached to lines created from plant fibers. Men also caught fish using sharp arrows and spears fashioned from wood and sharpened stones. Other fishers relied on wooden traps and nets woven together with plant fibers. People could fish from the riverbanks or while standing in shallow waters. Men also paddled out to deep waters and fished from their dugout canoes.

Hunting

In addition to fishing, men hunted to provide food and materials for their families. Hunting usually took men away from their homes and into the surrounding forests, where deer, rabbits, raccoons, and wild turkeys lived. A good hunter had to be patient, brave, and swift. He often tracked a fast-moving animal for hours before he was able to move close enough to hit it with an arrow. Small groups of hunters sometimes worked together to catch large animals such as deer. Small animals were caught in wooden traps and collected later.

Hearty meals

When men returned to their homes after successful fishing or hunting trips, they gave their catches to the women, who cleaned and stored all the useable parts and preserved the meat. Meat was dried by being smoked over a fire or in a **smokehouse**. A smokehouse was a small building that was kept full of smoke. Smoked fish and meat were added to stews, which simmered all day long. People ate some of the stew whenever they were hungry.

Some hunters wore deer skins, which allowed them to creep closer to deer without attracting attention.

Clothing from nature

Powhatan women used materials such as deer hides and plant fibers to handmake clothing for the men, women, and older children of their village. Babies and young children often wore no clothes at all.

Clothing for men and boys

Men and older boys wore **breechcloths**, which were made from rectangular pieces of soft deer hide or woven plant fibers. A man wore a breechcloth gathered between his legs and then pulled over a belt made from cord or a piece of hide. The ends of the breechcloth hung over in flaps covering the front of his thighs. When the weather became cool, Powhatan men and boys often attached deer-hide leggings to their belts. They rarely wore shirts, but some men of higher status wore **mantles**, or sleeveless coats.

Clothing for women and girls

Women usually wore plain dresses or skirts that hung from belts, similar to a male's breechcloth. Like men, women of higher status wore mantles that were decorated with shells and **embroidery**, or designs that were stitched into clothing.

Body decorations

Powhatan men and women decorated their bodies in several ways. They had tattoos on their bodies, often with images from nature. They also wore earrings and other jewelry made from animal bones, shells, and copper. For special occasions, men and women painted their shoulders with **pigments**, or plant dyes. Pigments were black, red, blue, yellow, or white. People added dust and feathers to the pigments to complete the designs. The colors and patterns were changed for various events.

Hairstyles and headwear

Girls who were too young to marry shaved off their hair in the front and at the sides with the sharp edges of shells. At about the age of twelve, they grew all their hair long. Boys and men usually wore their hair long. Hunters and warriors often shaved the right side of their heads to keep their hair from getting tangled while using bows to shoot arrows. During ceremonies, men and women wore beaded headbands that were adorned with feathers.

This chief wears a headdress made of dyed deer hair and feathers. A pounded copper plate hangs from the headdress.

Moccasins

Powhatan people wore footwear called moccasins only when they ventured into the forest. Each moccasin was formed from one piece of strong animal hide. The seams were sewn together with sinew.

*Powhatan moccasins were **puckered**, or gathered into folds, at the toes. People of some neighboring nations puckered their moccasins at the tops.*

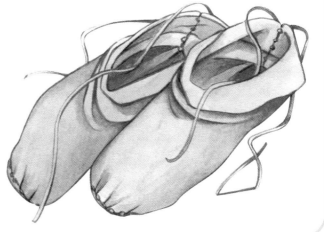

Handmade goods

The Powhatans were talented at making goods such as tools and household items from a variety of materials. Some materials required very little craftsmanship to be turned into useful everyday objects.

Expert skills were required to make other items properly. Many handcrafted objects were both functional and attractive. For example, once shells were cleaned, they could be used as spoonlike utensils. Most household items were made by women.

Pottery
Women mixed together wet clay, small pebbles, and ground-up shells to make pottery dishes and smoking pipes. Cord or netting was sometimes pressed into the outside of a piece of pottery to create a design. After an item was molded into the desired shape, it was left in the sun to dry. The pottery was later heated in a fire to increase its strength. Most pottery had thick walls and rough textures. Dishes were created in a range of shapes and sizes for various uses, such as holding food or collecting water.

Weaving
Powhatan women were highly skilled weavers. They wove sturdy, long-lasting mats, clothing, cords, and nets from plant materials. Women made items such as ceremonial masks and dolls by weaving materials such as corn husks. They also wove beautiful baskets using strong leaves, slender pieces of wood, and plant-fiber cord. The baskets were used to store food and other goods.

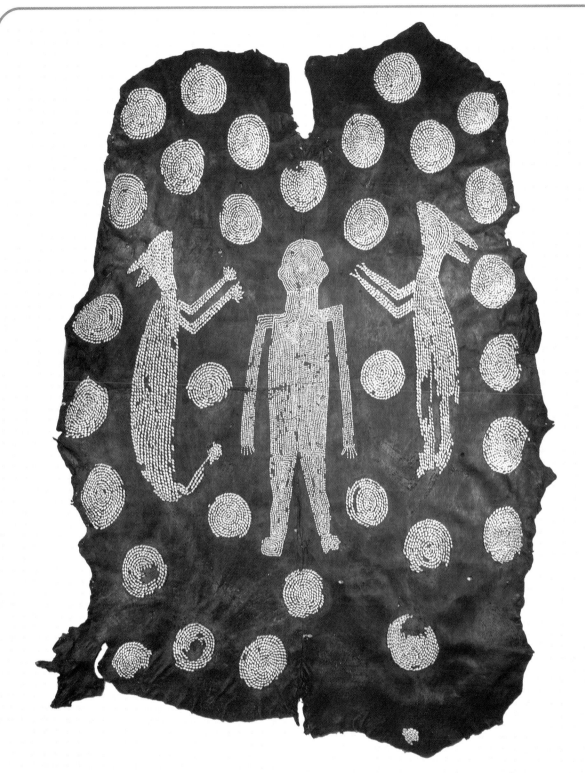

Beadwork

Powhatan craftspeople were known for their high-quality beadwork. They carefully sewed tiny shells onto clothing to create meaningful designs. The most famous example of Powhatan beadwork that still exists is shown above. It is the ceremonial mantle once worn by Wahunsonacock.

Preparing for adulthood

Powhatan children were included in the daily lives of the adults around them. Children learned about their history and culture by listening to the stories their elders told. From an early age, each child was taught the skills he or she would need to be a productive adult member of society. Even the children's simple toys were small versions of adult tools and weapons.

Daily activities

Babies spent their days strapped into **cradleboards**, which were wooden panels made comfortable with layers of hide and moss. Mothers carried the cradleboards around like backpacks. Once a child could walk, he or she was responsible for keeping up with his or her mother. By the age of three, girls and boys were included in various daily activities meant to prepare them for adulthood. Parents and relatives did not protect children from the many hardships of life. Instead, most hardships were believed to strengthen children. For example, parents bathed their children each day in the cold river to make them strong.

The lives of girls

Young girls helped their mothers farm, gather food, cook, make clothing and other goods, and construct homes. They were even skilled at many crafts. They learned how to behave and how to become good parents by **mimicking**, or acting like, their mothers. In their spare time, young girls played with dolls and practiced being mothers. When girls were about thirteen years old, they usually married and started their own families.

A boy's life

Before boys could join men on hunting or fishing expeditions, they had to prove themselves. They watched men craft tools and weapons. Parents encouraged their sons to make their own bows and arrows and practice shooting animals that came close to the village. A boy gained recognition from his family by bringing home meat for the stew pot. Fathers gave their sons new adult names after they proved themselves as hunters.

Huskanaw

When a boy ten years of age or older showed that he had special skills, he was sometimes tested in an initiation ceremony called *huskanaw*. Young leaders and warriors gathered the chosen boys in the forests outside their villages. The boys were isolated and given physical challenges. They ate certain plants that made them forget their former lives. This ordeal forced the boys to concentrate completely on becoming powerful healers and spiritual leaders who could ensure the survival of their nations. Young boys were considered wise men when they returned from huskanaw to their villages.

25

The story of Pocahontas

Ætatis suæ 21. A. 1616.

One Powhatan child continues to be famous hundreds of years after her lifetime. The legend of Pocahontas is well known because it involved some English settlers. The true details of Pocohantas' short life are fascinating, even though historians believe she is remembered for an event that never happened.

As a child

Pocahontas was born sometime around 1595. She was one of Wahunsonacock's many children. She was given the name Matoaka, but later she received the nickname Pocahontas, which means "naughty child." When settlers from England arrived in the Tidewater region in 1607, Pocahontas was about twelve years old.

The capture of John Smith

At first, Wahunsonacock and his people were friendly with the English settlers. The Native people provided the newcomers with food and showed them how to survive in the wilderness. The relationship between the two groups grew hostile, however, as the English demanded more food and land. In 1608, a **colonist** named Captain John Smith was captured by the Powhatans. Smith later claimed that he was rescued by Pocahontas, who begged her father to spare Smith's life. Many historians believe, however, that Smith was simply involved in a ceremony adopting him into Powhatan culture.

Kidnapped

Several years later, the conflicts between the Powhatans and the English became even more of a problem. To gain control over Wahunsonacock, English colonists kidnapped Pocahontas. They took her to Jamestown, where she was held prisoner for about a year. While living with the foreigners, Pocahontas learned their customs and took the name Rebecca.

A wedding

Pocahontas met English colonist John Rolfe during her time in Jamestown. Her imprisonment ended in 1614, when she married Rolfe. The painting below shows their wedding ceremony. Shortly afterward, the couple had a son named Thomas.

A trip to England

The marriage of Pocohantas and John Rolfe encouraged peace between the Powhatans and the settlers. In the spring of 1616, a tobacco company paid for the Rolfe family to travel to England in order to create interest for the new **colony** among the English people. While in England, Pocahontas was treated like royalty because her father was described as a king. She even met with King James and his court. A year later, while Pocahontas was on board a ship for the return trip to Virginia, she became very ill. She left the ship at the English port of Gravesend, where she died at the age of 21. John Rolfe and his son later returned to Virginia.

Just a year after Pocahontas died in England, Wahunsonacock also died. Their deaths marked the end of the harmony between the Powhatans and the English. Many colonists wanted to increase the size of their profitable tobacco farms. They believed they had the right to claim ownership of large pieces of Powhatan territory. The Powhatans felt that outsiders had no right to take over the territories on which their people had lived and hunted for years. Many conflicts erupted as a result of the disagreements between the two groups. In the following three decades, hundreds of people from both sides lost their lives in brutal attacks.

Opechancanough's reign

Wahunsonacock's brother Opitchapam inherited the leadership role of mamanatowick. He was soon replaced by the powerful Opechancanough, another of Wahunsonacock's brothers. Opechancanough had previously been the werowance of the influential Pamunkey nation. He was distressed by the raids on Native villages that were carried out by the settlers. In 1622, Opechancanough led his warriors in a series of counterattacks against English settlements. The fierce attacks and counterattacks continued until the mid-1630s, when both sides grew too weak to fight.

The colonists take control

By the mid-1600s, there were fewer than 5,000 members of the Powhatan nations left in the Tidewater region. The colonists brought with them many diseases to which the Powhatans had never been exposed. Thousands of Powhatans died of illnesses such as smallpox. Those who survived the illnesses had their traditional ways of life destroyed. To take power away from the Powhatan chiefdom, the governor of Virginia began **appointing** Native leaders in 1665.

Hereditary leaders, who traditionally would have led their people, lost power within 50 years. By the early 1700s, most Powhatan nations were moved to small **reservations** that did not have enough food sources or natural materials necessary for survival. At the end of the 1700s, the Accomac and the Pamunkey nations were the only members of the Powhatan chiefdom to be recognized officially as Native groups by the Virginian government. Many of the other nations were wiped out or forced out of the area.

Opechancanough's defeat

At 80 years of age, Opechancanough led another attack against the English colonists in 1644. That year, the colonists captured the Powhatan leader and shot him after he refused to sign a **treaty** with them. Opechancanough's death led to the defeat and ultimate destruction of the Powhatan chiefdom.

This painting depicts Opechancanough as he convinces his people to attack the colonists.

Changed lives

Over time, the Powhatan people were forced to stop fishing, hunting, and gathering for survival. Instead, many took on work as guides and servants in the colonies. They left their villages and moved to the new towns and cities that sprang up across the country. Gradually, the Powhatans conformed to fit in with colonial, and later, American society.

Life today

Many **descendants** of the survivors from the Powhatan nations eventually returned to the Tidewater region or settled in nearby states. Seven of the nations, with a total of about 10,000 members, are currently recognized by the federal government. These people are a vital link in the history of the United States of America. They strive to honor the traditions of their ancestors and to teach younger generations the history of their nations. What remains of the Powhatan language is preserved through English writings from the 1600s. The Powhatan language is taught to Native children today.

Many present-day Powhatans participate in some of the same festivals and ceremonies celebrated by their ancestors. Dancing, shown right, is part of these celebrations.

Find out more!

There are many fascinating websites that describe the lives of the Powhatans, their interactions with the Jamestown colonists, and how they live today. Check out the links below or type "Powhatan" into your favorite Internet search engine.

- www.powhatan.org
- www.mariner.org/chesapeakebay/native/nam002.html
- www.ab.mec.edu/jamestown/powhatan.html

Glossary

Note: Boldfaced words that are defined in the book may not appear in the glossary.

ancestor A person, usually farther back in a family's history than grandparents, from whom someone is descended

appoint To select a person to fill a position

colonist A person who lives in a colony

colony An area ruled by a faraway country

descendant A person who comes from a particular ancestor or group of ancestors

hereditary Describing a position into which a person is born

language family A group of languages that are similar to one another

lifeways The customs, activities, and traditions involved in the way a group of people live their day-to-day lives

longhouse A long dwelling built of poles and bark that is shared by many people, especially Native people who lived in the eastern Great Lakes region

nutrients Ingredients in the soil that help plants grow

reservation A specific area of land set aside by a government for Native people

sapling A young tree

settler A person who moves to a new place and makes it his or her home

sinew The strong connective tissue of animals, dried for use as string or thread

territory An area of land and water on which a group of people traditionally lived, hunted, fished, and gathered food

treaty A contract or agreement

Index

1 2 3 4 5 6 7 8 9 0 Printed in the U.S.A. 4 3 2 1 0 9 8 7 6 5